To Michele,
Journal your dream reality.

love
Michele xx

Prosperity
JOURNAL

♥

© Copyright 2019 Michele Walsh

Dream Believe Attract

All content is original by Michele Walsh.

All rights reserved.

No part of this book may be reproduced either by mechanical, photographic, scanned or distributed in any printed or electronic for without permission.

Cover Design by Vicki Nicolson, Brand Creative

For more information, visit: www.michelewalsh.com

DISCLAIMER: Although the author has made every effort to ensure that the information in this book was correct at press time, the author does not assume and hereby disclaim any liability to any party for any loss, damage or disruption caused by errors or omissions, whether such errors or omissions result from negligence, accident or any other cause. This book is not intended to substitute for the medical advice of physicians. The reader should consult a physician in matters relating to his/her health, and particularity with respect to any symptoms that may require diagnoses or medical attention. The methods described within this book are the author's personal interpretations. They are not intended to be a definitive set of instructions for this project. You may discover there are other methods and materials to accomplish the same end result.

Time to manifest your dreams...

Before you begin...

Is there such a thing, can you literally manifest anything you want?

Well you manifested this very journal you hold in your hands!

Over the years I have helped 1000's of women manifest magnificent things, I noticed that my clients were buying journals but many seemed so complicated and overwhelming.

This journal is designed to be simple but effective. Something you can have on your desk, carry with you and use to follow your magical journey of manifesting.

I have created this to help you get energy and mindset alignment plus giving you the awareness of exactly how you can manifest. You are manifesting 24/7 anyway but I want you to focus your thoughts into consciously manifesting ONLY the things you want.

Life doesn't happen to you, it happens because of you - your thoughts, your feelings, your actions and most importantly your energy are radiating a frequency that is attracting it's exact match. Raising your energy and your vibration will attract amazing opportunities to you that previously you only dreamt about.

I know how much of a chore journaling can feel like, another thing on your 'to do' list but I want to transform your experience so this Manifesting Journal you hold in your hands becomes your secret best friend.

I want it to become your support when you are doubting yourself, your safe place to pour out your hearts desires and a record of all the magnificent things you are manifesting on a daily basis.

I want to help you make conscious manifesting unconscious so that you don't have to focus and concentrate on doing things in a certain way, for a certain length of time to guarantee 100% success. You already have 100% success in manifesting but here and now I want to direct that to only the things you want.

The Power of this Journal ...

This journal you hold in your hands has the power to change your world

The sooner you start the quicker your magical manifesting journey begins

This is a distinctly obvious statement but to get the most out of this journal you have to actually use it. How many journals have never made it our of your desk or drawer? Make sure this doesn't happen to this one!

I know you are time deficient, there are so many demands on your time but by putting aside just 10 minutes a day will transform your business and life beyond belief. I have made this so simple, straight forward, easy to use and easy to incorporate into a simple daily routine.

In this journal I am sharing the exact steps that I have shared with 1000's of clients over more that 10 years and who have gone on to manifest incredible results in their life and business.

Keep this journal where you can see it, follow the simple daily basics to allow manifesting to work for you.

Adjust your course. Manifesting is specific to you, you need to feel your way.

Manifesting is an awareness that is already inside of you but has been buried by our modern way of living. A way that no longer serves you or helps you manifest everything you want.

Manifesting is all about using the power of your emotions and vision to accelerate the manifesting process. Your focus is to live in joy, happiness, contentment, excitement and all the other high vibration emotions that will radiate out from you to magnetise your hearts desire.

Underpromise and over deliver on your own personal expectations. To start the journal on the first Monday after you receive it. Set aside 10 minutes a day just to get started.

Place your Prosperity Journal where you can see it and make it your companion that you will love.

This journal has been created from a place of pure love and I want you to receive and use it with the same power of emotions.

Love it as you would a best friend. A friend that looks out for you, that has your best interest at heart and that want's only the best for you.

You have so much abundance to claim in your lifetime.

Let the journey begin right here and right now.

How to Make the Most of This Journal

As someone who has dipped in and out of using journals the one big thing that has put me off is thinking I need to write in it everyday. If you're anything like me some days you just feel like pouring it all out and some days you don't.

The great news is unlike most journals, there are absolutely no rules to using this journal. This is because you are the creator of everything in your life and the best way to create everything you desire is only to do the things you LOVE including journaling.

This journal was initially created to support clients on my Path of Prosperity Program but it will give all women globally the chance to put basic manifesting steps into place on a daily basis and be open and ready to receive the life you're meant to be living.

The basics of this journal are whatever it means to you, it doesn't matter if your beliefs are in religion, spirit, angels or something else I think you know there is a higher power than you at work trying to work through you. If you can still your mind long enough you will hear the guidance of your next steps along a path that will bring your dreams and desires to life.

You can start this journal on any day of any month in any year. All you need to do is put the date at the top of the page on the day you are journaling. There is a double page per day but if that's not enough there are extra pages at the back of the journal, called Mega Journaling.

Meditation will change your world, if you are not currently meditating then you are missing a whole piece that can make your manifesting journey easier.

Meditation quietens the mind and allows you to hear guided action to take you in the direction of manifesting your dreams and prosperity.

Meditation can take many forms and it's whatever is right for you, there is no right or wrong way. It can be listening to a guided meditation*, just being quiet, going for a walk, running, in fact anything where you are able to be in the moment and think of nothing.

Gratitude is another fast track to accelerating your manifesting power.

Gratitude shouldn't be a chore, something you need to tick off your to do list but something you should feel in every fibre of your being. Again you can choose to do your gratitude in anyway that fits with you.

One of the most effective things you can do is write in the journal pages, say it out loud and then finish with a flourish of 5 thank you's. You can say/think what you're grateful for before you get up in a morning or do it last thing at night and if you really want to max out on super high vibration of gratitude then do it morning and evening, everyday.

One thing is for sure when you incorporate meditation and gratitude into your daily life then you are definitely getting into alignment and allowing a higher power to work through you.

To help you keep track there are icons at the bottom of the right hand page which you can tick if you have done them that day.

Lots of Love,

Michele

"Here starts the journey to making all my dreams come true..."

Your Journaling Symbols

When you see the images below take note if you have managed to complete them in your daily life. These symbols are threaded throughout the journal to bring you back to your awareness of how important they are to manifesting

Gratitude: finish your days with a flourish of five Thank You's

*****Meditation:** tap into your higher power and intuition daily

Journal: a page for everyday to pour your daily musings, dreams and manifestations

Visit: www.Michelewalsh.com/Journalbonuses for your free manifesting meditation

Your Energy and Vibration

The most important thing for you to understand about manifesting is that the Universe is responding to your thoughts, feelings, beliefs, energy and vibration. Like a highly tuned machine when you synchronise all these you have hit the sweet spot in your journey of manifestation.

Your most important focus of the day is to monitor and adjust accordingly your energy and vibration. What you think affects what you feel which sends out a vibration from you throughout the Universe and attracts exactly that which matches it.

The quickest way to manifest your desires is be specific and measurable in what you want to attract.

You can have monthly, weekly or daily desires, just ensure they're all part of the bigger picture. You have to be in alignment with that which you desire, take time each day to write out your desires. Replicate our ancestors who have put pen to paper for thousands of years, confirming your declarations to the Universe.

Vision of My Dream Business and Life

There is no separation when you have your dream business you will create your dream life. Write out the details of your dream business and life, in the present tense, as if you are living it now. Be descriptive in the details; how will you feel, how will things look, how you live in all aspects of your dream life. Who will you surround yourself with, what will you do on a daily, weekly, regular basis that makes up all aspects of your dream business and life. Make your words come to life so that your mind creates a compelling vision that you will want to read over and over again until it appears in your life.

The Basics of Manifesting

Clarity
Be specific in what you want to manifest.

Align
Your beliefs with your desires.

Guided Action
Listen to your intuition about what to do next.

Let Go
Of the how your manifestation is going to come to you.

Positive Expectation
Of your desire coming 100% non negotiable.

Magical Manifesting Month of

Reality Creation + Manifestation
Frederick Dodson - Scripting

Things I want to manifest this month...

Be creative, Act as if, Scripting
Explore "What if"

Creating an outcome story to release Sheila
Releasing the block for calling people
Start with Who am I, Where am I, When is it
What do I want, Why, How, What do I need to overcome,
How does it feel to overcome that.
Rescript the past, Script the future
Act as if...

Best friends with Angie, Sheila's daughter
we grew up together and enjoyed the passion
of dancing. I've gone to see Sheila to help her
review services and save money. I am new to
this business but feel confident. I have shown
them the best achievable savings but Bust
is not happy to change the BB and Sheila
wants to stay with her PAYG. I change the
figures by recalculating and show her the

difference. We also take into account the boiler cover she will be saving each month £9 as not needed.

Sheila says she is happy to switch stuff and trust me because she knows me. I reassure her that we and I will deal with things and she can call me for help.

A couple of months pass and Sheila realises that the DD is more than she was paying and I explain that she had overpayed previously and built up so much credit that they paid her a lump sum when she switched. I offered to investigate and after many conversations and meter readings a picture was emerging that estimations had created a debit balance.

I put my heart and soul into getting a good outcome but developed a fear that I had let her down and ruined my reputation with her and her family. I am sorry if my inexperience caused you anxiety

Daily Gratitude For What I Have

Date 6/6/20

I am happy and grateful that I have…

THE NEW SCRIPT

I am Michele UW distributer, successfully growing a service to many people, helping them to bring simplicity to their lives and bringing more money into their homes.

I have helped Sheila and Burt look at the savings they can make by adding the broadband to reduce the energy cost. They have decided to get our smart meter and will get the £50 credit. They feel reassured that I have their best interests at heart and love the face that they can come to me for help because they trust me.

They have referred many of theyre dancing friends who I have also helped to become happy customers.

Angie was so impressed that Max has decided to join too.

Daily Gratitude For What I Want   Date 6/6/20

I am happy and grateful that I have manifested...

My beautiful bedroom and place of peace. I have a loving family and everyone is safe and well through this pandemic.

I am opening up my mind an heart to the laws of attraction through the access I have to learning materials

We have a large home and garden and are not constrained

I love the freedom I have daily and always have more than enough money, abundance of food and love in my life.

I enjoy the space and time to explore my spiritual journey

Thank You Source.

 I tapped into your higher power and intuition today through meditation ☐

Daily Gratitude For What I Have   Date... 6/6/20

I am happy and grateful that I have...

A free mind that is calm and looks for the good in all.

Angels around me to share their knowledge and wisdom and provide a loving presence and tell me daily what I need to know.

I share my life with a thoughtful and loving partner and a sensitive and loving son. My adult children are happy in their choice of partners and are living their chosen lives.

I am grateful my elderly parents are fit and healthy and happy.

I am grateful for my working opportunities that bring money into me both easily and effortlessly and provide a passive, residual flow of money regularly

Daily Gratitude For What I Want   Date........................

I am happy and grateful that I have manifested...

....
....
....
....
....
....
....
....
....
....
....
....
....
....
....

 I tapped into your higher power and intuition today through meditation ☐

Daily Gratitude For What I Have   Date... 2/11/26

I am happy and grateful that I have...

My blessings.
I am healthy — mobile, breath easily
I can see, hear, touch, smell, taste
My parents are healthy
My children are healthy and loving
My partner is thoughtful and loving
My partner is well and improving his food health choices.
We have a mortgage free home, a lot of space, central heating and warmth protection from the weather
I have a lovely room and comfortable bed. I have freedom of choice in my day.
I have abundance of money in the bank
Income that flows in effortlessly
I have the best opportunity right now to help people through difficult times

Daily Gratitude For What I Want

Date: 13/12/20

I am happy and grateful that I have manifested...

I am courageous because of you Lord Jesus
I am a good listener because of you Jesus
I am patient because of you Lord Jesus
I am attentive because of you Lord Jesus
I am successful because of you Lord Jesus
I am secure because of you Lord Jesus
I am happy because of you Lord Jesus
I am loving because of you Lord Jesus
I am peaceful because of you Lord Jesus
I am healthy because of you Lord Jesus
I am a helper because of you Lord Jesus
I am safe because of you Lord Jesus
I am protected because of you Lord Jesus
I am loved because of you Lord Jesus
I am satisfied because of you Lord Jesus
I am strong because of you Lord Jesus
I am an achiever because of you Lord Jesus

 I tapped into your higher power and intuition today through meditation

Daily Gratitude For What I Have   Date...19th May 23

I am happy and grateful that I have...

Climbing into bed a couple of mins before midnight

Feeling a distinct lack of JOY and ask "What's it all about?"

"Why do I lack compassion?"

"Am I... in Charlotte's words... Passive aggressive in character?"

"In limbo, getting nowhere with everything"

Life's journey feels like a trudge through treacle

But... I am blessed in many ways

Daily Gratitude For What I Want

Date..........................

I am happy and grateful that I have manifested...

....

....

....

....

....

....

....

....

....

....

....

....

....

....

....

 I tapped into your higher power and intuition today through meditation ☐

Daily Gratitude For What I Have   Date..........................

I am happy and grateful that I have...

Daily Gratitude For What I Want Date..........................

I am happy and grateful that I have manifested...

....
....
....
....
....
....
....
....
....
....
....
....
....
....
....
....

 I tapped into your higher power and intuition today through meditation ☐

Daily Gratitude For What I Have   Date..........................

I am happy and grateful that I have...

Daily Gratitude For What I Want Date........................

I am happy and grateful that I have manifested...

....

....

....

....

....

....

....

....

....

....

....

....

....

....

....

 I tapped into your higher power and intuition today through meditation ☐

Daily Gratitude For What I Have

Date..........................

I am happy and grateful that I have...

Daily Gratitude For What I Want   Date..........................

I am happy and grateful that I have manifested...

....

....

....

....

....

....

....

....

....

....

....

....

....

....

 I tapped into your higher power and intuition today through meditation ☐

Daily Gratitude For What I Have Date..........................

I am happy and grateful that I have...

Daily Gratitude For What I Want   Date..........................

I am happy and grateful that I have manifested...

....

....

....

....

....

....

....

....

....

....

....

....

....

....

....

....

 I tapped into your higher power and intuition today through meditation ☐

Daily Gratitude For What I Have

Date..........................

I am happy and grateful that I have...

Daily Gratitude For What I Want Date..........................

I am happy and grateful that I have manifested...

 I tapped into your higher power and intuition today through meditation ☐

Daily Gratitude For What I Have

Date..........................

I am happy and grateful that I have...

Daily Gratitude For What I Want   Date..........................

I am happy and grateful that I have manifested...

....
....
....
....
....
....
....
....
....
....
....
....
....
....
....

 I tapped into your higher power and intuition today through meditation ☐

"I am the creator of the prosperity I desire."

Magical Manifesting Month of

Things I want to manifest this month...

Daily Gratitude For What I Have   Date..........................

I am happy and grateful that I have...

Daily Gratitude For What I Want   Date..........................

I am happy and grateful that I have manifested...

 I tapped into your higher power and intuition today through meditation ☐

Daily Gratitude For What I Have　　　　Date..........................

I am happy and grateful that I have...

Daily Gratitude For What I Want   Date..........................

I am happy and grateful that I have manifested...

....

....

....

....

....

....

....

....

....

....

....

....

....

....

 I tapped into your higher power and intuition today through meditation ☐

Daily Gratitude For What I Have

Date..........................

I am happy and grateful that I have...

Daily Gratitude For What I Want   Date..........................

I am happy and grateful that I have manifested...

 I tapped into your higher power and intuition today through meditation ☐

Daily Gratitude For What I Have Date..........................

I am happy and grateful that I have...

Daily Gratitude For What I Want   Date........................

I am happy and grateful that I have manifested...

....

....

....

....

....

....

....

....

....

....

....

....

....

....

 I tapped into your higher power and intuition today through meditation ☐

Daily Gratitude For What I Have   Date..........................

I am happy and grateful that I have...

....

....

....

....

....

....

....

....

....

....

....

....

....

....

....

....

....

Daily Gratitude For What I Want

Date..........................

I am happy and grateful that I have manifested...

....

....

....

....

....

....

....

....

....

....

....

....

....

....

 I tapped into your higher power and intuition today through meditation ☐

Daily Gratitude For What I Have

Date..........................

I am happy and grateful that I have...

Daily Gratitude For What I Want

Date..........................

I am happy and grateful that I have manifested...

....

....

....

....

....

....

....

....

....

....

....

....

....

....

....

 I tapped into your higher power and intuition today through meditation ☐

Daily Gratitude For What I Have

Date..........................

I am happy and grateful that I have...

Daily Gratitude For What I Want   Date..........................

I am happy and grateful that I have manifested...

 I tapped into your higher power and intuition today through meditation ☐

Daily Gratitude For What I Have   Date..........................

I am happy and grateful that I have...

Daily Gratitude For What I Want   Date........................

I am happy and grateful that I have manifested...

....

....

....

....

....

....

....

....

....

....

....

....

....

....

 I tapped into your higher power and intuition today through meditation ☐

Daily Gratitude For What I Have　　　　Date..........................

I am happy and grateful that I have...

Daily Gratitude For What I Want   Date........................

I am happy and grateful that I have manifested...

....
....
....
....
....
....
....
....
....
....
....
....
....
....
....

 I tapped into your higher power and intuition today through meditation ☐

Daily Gratitude For What I Have   Date..........................

I am happy and grateful that I have...

Daily Gratitude For What I Want

Date..........................

I am happy and grateful that I have manifested...

....

....

....

....

....

....

....

....

....

....

....

....

....

....

 I tapped into your higher power and intuition today through meditation ☐

"My vibration matches all I desire."

Magical Manifesting Month of

....

Things I want to manifest this month...

 **Daily Gratitude For What I Have**   Date..........................

I am happy and grateful that I have...

Daily Gratitude For What I Want Date..........................

I am happy and grateful that I have manifested...

....

....

....

....

....

....

....

....

....

....

....

....

....

....

 I tapped into your higher power and intuition today through meditation ☐

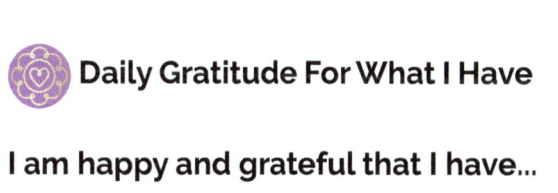

Daily Gratitude For What I Have

Date..........................

I am happy and grateful that I have...

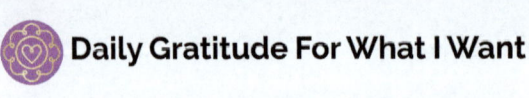 **Daily Gratitude For What I Want**   Date..........................

I am happy and grateful that I have manifested...

 I tapped into your higher power and intuition today through meditation ☐

 **Daily Gratitude For What I Have**   Date..........................

I am happy and grateful that I have...

Daily Gratitude For What I Want Date..........................

I am happy and grateful that I have manifested...

 I tapped into your higher power and intuition today through meditation ☐

Daily Gratitude For What I Have　　　　Date..........................

I am happy and grateful that I have...

Daily Gratitude For What I Want   Date..........................

I am happy and grateful that I have manifested...

....
....
....
....
....
....
....
....
....
....
....
....
....
....

 I tapped into your higher power and intuition today through meditation ☐

Daily Gratitude For What I Have Date..........................

I am happy and grateful that I have...

Daily Gratitude For What I Want   Date........................

I am happy and grateful that I have manifested...

 I tapped into your higher power and intuition today through meditation ☐

Daily Gratitude For What I Have　　　　Date..........................

I am happy and grateful that I have...

Daily Gratitude For What I Want   Date........................

I am happy and grateful that I have manifested...

_____

_____

_____

_____

_____

_____

_____

_____

_____

_____

_____

_____

_____

_____

_____

 I tapped into your higher power and intuition today through meditation ☐

Daily Gratitude For What I Have   Date..........................

I am happy and grateful that I have...

Daily Gratitude For What I Want Date..........................

I am happy and grateful that I have manifested...

....

....

....

....

....

....

....

....

....

....

....

....

....

....

 I tapped into your higher power and intuition today through meditation ☐

Daily Gratitude For What I Have   Date..........................

I am happy and grateful that I have...

Daily Gratitude For What I Want   Date........................

I am happy and grateful that I have manifested...

....
....
....
....
....
....
....
....
....
....
....
....
....
....
....

 I tapped into your higher power and intuition today through meditation ☐

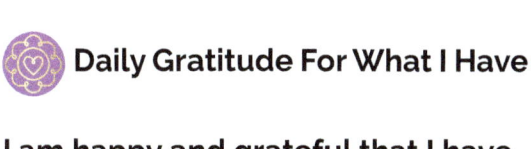 **Daily Gratitude For What I Have**   Date..........................

I am happy and grateful that I have...

Daily Gratitude For What I Want Date..........................

I am happy and grateful that I have manifested...

_____

_____

_____

_____

_____

_____

_____

_____

_____

_____

_____

_____

_____

_____

 I tapped into your higher power and intuition today through meditation ☐

Daily Gratitude For What I Have

Date..........................

I am happy and grateful that I have...

Daily Gratitude For What I Want   Date..........................

I am happy and grateful that I have manifested...

....

....

....

....

....

....

....

....

....

....

....

....

....

....

....

 I tapped into your higher power and intuition today through meditation ☐

"Dream it.
Believe it.
Attract it."

Magical Manifesting Month of

Things I want to manifest this month...

Daily Gratitude For What I Have

Date..........................

I am happy and grateful that I have...

Daily Gratitude For What I Want   Date........................

I am happy and grateful that I have manifested...

 I tapped into your higher power and intuition today through meditation ☐

 **Daily Gratitude For What I Have**   Date..........................

I am happy and grateful that I have...

Daily Gratitude For What I Want

Date..........................

I am happy and grateful that I have manifested...

....
....
....
....
....
....
....
....
....
....
....
....
....
....
....

 I tapped into your higher power and intuition today through meditation ☐

Daily Gratitude For What I Have   Date………………………

I am happy and grateful that I have…

Daily Gratitude For What I Want   Date..........................

I am happy and grateful that I have manifested...

....

....

....

....

....

....

....

....

....

....

....

....

....

....

 I tapped into your higher power and intuition today through meditation ☐

Daily Gratitude For What I Have   Date..........................

I am happy and grateful that I have...

Daily Gratitude For What I Want   Date..........................

I am happy and grateful that I have manifested...

 I tapped into your higher power and intuition today through meditation ☐

Daily Gratitude For What I Have   Date..........................

I am happy and grateful that I have...

Daily Gratitude For What I Want Date.........................

I am happy and grateful that I have manifested...

....

....

....

....

....

....

....

....

....

....

....

....

....

....

....

 I tapped into your higher power and intuition today through meditation ☐

Daily Gratitude For What I Have   Date..........................

I am happy and grateful that I have...

Daily Gratitude For What I Want   Date..........................

I am happy and grateful that I have manifested...

_____
_____
_____
_____
_____
_____
_____
_____
_____
_____
_____
_____
_____
_____
_____

 I tapped into your higher power and intuition today through meditation ☐

Daily Gratitude For What I Have

Date..........................

I am happy and grateful that I have...

Daily Gratitude For What I Want   Date..........................

I am happy and grateful that I have manifested...

....

....

....

....

....

....

....

....

....

....

....

....

....

....

 I tapped into your higher power and intuition today through meditation ☐

Daily Gratitude For What I Have   Date..........................

I am happy and grateful that I have...

Daily Gratitude For What I Want   Date..........................

I am happy and grateful that I have manifested...

....
....
....
....
....
....
....
....
....
....
....
....
....
....

 I tapped into your higher power and intuition today through meditation ☐

Daily Gratitude For What I Have   Date..........................

I am happy and grateful that I have...

Daily Gratitude For What I Want Date.........................

I am happy and grateful that I have manifested...

....

....

....

....

....

....

....

....

....

....

....

....

....

....

 I tapped into your higher power and intuition today through meditation ☐

Daily Gratitude For What I Have   Date..........................

I am happy and grateful that I have...

Daily Gratitude For What I Want   Date...........................

I am happy and grateful that I have manifested...

 I tapped into your higher power and intuition today through meditation ☐

"I tap into my infinite potential daily."

Magical Manifesting Month of

....

Things I want to manifest this month...

Daily Gratitude For What I Have

Date..........................

I am happy and grateful that I have...

Daily Gratitude For What I Want   Date..........................

I am happy and grateful that I have manifested...

 I tapped into your higher power and intuition today through meditation ☐

Daily Gratitude For What I Have Date..........................

I am happy and grateful that I have...

Daily Gratitude For What I Want   Date........................

I am happy and grateful that I have manifested...

....

....

....

....

....

....

....

....

....

....

....

....

....

....

....

 I tapped into your higher power and intuition today through meditation ☐

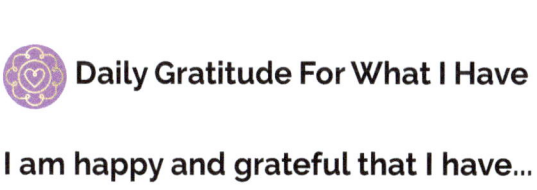
Daily Gratitude For What I Have

Date..........................

I am happy and grateful that I have...

Daily Gratitude For What I Want   Date..........................

I am happy and grateful that I have manifested...

_____

_____

_____

_____

_____

_____

_____

_____

_____

_____

_____

_____

_____

_____

 I tapped into your higher power and intuition today through meditation ☐

Daily Gratitude For What I Have

Date..........................

I am happy and grateful that I have...

Daily Gratitude For What I Want   Date..........................

I am happy and grateful that I have manifested...

 I tapped into your higher power and intuition today through meditation ☐

Daily Gratitude For What I Have Date..........................

I am happy and grateful that I have...

Daily Gratitude For What I Want   Date........................

I am happy and grateful that I have manifested...

....
....
....
....
....
....
....
....
....
....
....
....
....
....
....
....

 I tapped into your higher power and intuition today through meditation ☐

Daily Gratitude For What I Have   Date..........................

I am happy and grateful that I have...

Daily Gratitude For What I Want   Date........................

I am happy and grateful that I have manifested...

_____

_____

_____

_____

_____

_____

_____

_____

_____

_____

_____

_____

_____

_____

 I tapped into your higher power and intuition today through meditation ☐

Daily Gratitude For What I Have

Date..........................

I am happy and grateful that I have...

Daily Gratitude For What I Want   Date..........................

I am happy and grateful that I have manifested...

_____

_____

_____

_____

_____

_____

_____

_____

_____

_____

_____

_____

_____

_____

 I tapped into your higher power and intuition today through meditation ☐

Daily Gratitude For What I Have   Date..........................

I am happy and grateful that I have...

Daily Gratitude For What I Want   Date..........................

I am happy and grateful that I have manifested...

 I tapped into your higher power and intuition today through meditation ☐

Daily Gratitude For What I Have

Date..........................

I am happy and grateful that I have...

Daily Gratitude For What I Want   Date..........................

I am happy and grateful that I have manifested...

 I tapped into your higher power and intuition today through meditation ☐

 **Daily Gratitude For What I Have**   Date..........................

I am happy and grateful that I have...

Daily Gratitude For What I Want   Date........................

I am happy and grateful that I have manifested...

 I tapped into your higher power and intuition today through meditation ☐

"The perfect time to manifest my desires is now."

Magical Manifesting Month of

Things I want to manifest this month...

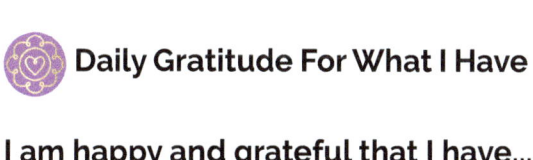 **Daily Gratitude For What I Have**   Date..........................

I am happy and grateful that I have...

Daily Gratitude For What I Want

Date..........................

I am happy and grateful that I have manifested...

....

....

....

....

....

....

....

....

....

....

....

....

....

....

....

 I tapped into your higher power and intuition today through meditation ☐

 **Daily Gratitude For What I Have**   Date..........................

I am happy and grateful that I have...

....

....

....

....

....

....

....

....

....

....

....

....

....

....

....

....

....

Daily Gratitude For What I Want   Date..........................

I am happy and grateful that I have manifested...

....
....
....
....
....
....
....
....
....
....
....
....
....
....
....

 I tapped into your higher power and intuition today through meditation ☐

Daily Gratitude For What I Have   Date..........................

I am happy and grateful that I have...

Daily Gratitude For What I Want   Date........................

I am happy and grateful that I have manifested...

 I tapped into your higher power and intuition today through meditation ☐

Daily Gratitude For What I Have　　　　Date............................

I am happy and grateful that I have...

Daily Gratitude For What I Want   Date..........................

I am happy and grateful that I have manifested...

 I tapped into your higher power and intuition today through meditation ☐

 **Daily Gratitude For What I Have**　　　　Date..........................

I am happy and grateful that I have...

Daily Gratitude For What I Want Date..........................

I am happy and grateful that I have manifested...

....
....
....
....
....
....
....
....
....
....
....
....
....
....
....

 I tapped into your higher power and intuition today through meditation ☐

Daily Gratitude For What I Have

Date..........................

I am happy and grateful that I have...

Daily Gratitude For What I Want   Date..........................

I am happy and grateful that I have manifested...

I tapped into your higher power and intuition today through meditation ☐

Daily Gratitude For What I Have   Date..........................

I am happy and grateful that I have...

Daily Gratitude For What I Want   Date..........................

I am happy and grateful that I have manifested...

 I tapped into your higher power and intuition today through meditation ☐

Daily Gratitude For What I Have   Date..........................

I am happy and grateful that I have...

Daily Gratitude For What I Want

Date..........................

I am happy and grateful that I have manifested...

....
....
....
....
....
....
....
....
....
....
....
....
....
....
....

 I tapped into your higher power and intuition today through meditation ☐

 **Daily Gratitude For What I Have**   Date..........................

I am happy and grateful that I have...

Daily Gratitude For What I Want   Date........................

I am happy and grateful that I have manifested...

 I tapped into your higher power and intuition today through meditation ☐

Daily Gratitude For What I Have   Date..........................

I am happy and grateful that I have...

Daily Gratitude For What I Want   Date............................

I am happy and grateful that I have manifested...

....

....

....

....

....

....

....

....

....

....

....

....

....

....

....

 I tapped into your higher power and intuition today through meditation ☐

"I am open to receive a miracle today."

Magical Manifesting Month of

....

Things I want to manifest this month...

 **Daily Gratitude For What I Have**   Date..........................

I am happy and grateful that I have...

Daily Gratitude For What I Want

Date..........................

I am happy and grateful that I have manifested...

 I tapped into your higher power and intuition today through meditation ☐

Daily Gratitude For What I Have   Date..........................

I am happy and grateful that I have...

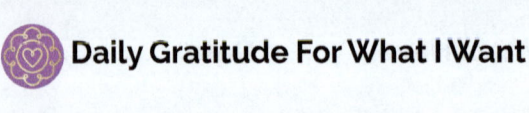 **Daily Gratitude For What I Want**   Date..........................

I am happy and grateful that I have manifested...

....
....
....
....
....
....
....
....
....
....
....
....
....
....

 I tapped into your higher power and intuition today through meditation ☐

 **Daily Gratitude For What I Have**   Date..........................

I am happy and grateful that I have...

Daily Gratitude For What I Want   Date..........................

I am happy and grateful that I have manifested...

....

....

....

....

....

....

....

....

....

....

....

....

....

....

....

 I tapped into your higher power and intuition today through meditation ☐

Daily Gratitude For What I Have

Date..........................

I am happy and grateful that I have...

Daily Gratitude For What I Want   Date..........................

I am happy and grateful that I have manifested...

 I tapped into your higher power and intuition today through meditation ☐

Daily Gratitude For What I Have　　　　Date..........................

I am happy and grateful that I have...

Daily Gratitude For What I Want Date..........................

I am happy and grateful that I have manifested...

....

....

....

....

....

....

....

....

....

....

....

....

....

....

....

....

....

 I tapped into your higher power and intuition today through meditation ☐

 **Daily Gratitude For What I Have** Date..........................

I am happy and grateful that I have...

Daily Gratitude For What I Want

Date..........................

I am happy and grateful that I have manifested...

_____
_____
_____
_____
_____
_____
_____
_____
_____
_____
_____
_____
_____
_____
_____

 I tapped into your higher power and intuition today through meditation ☐

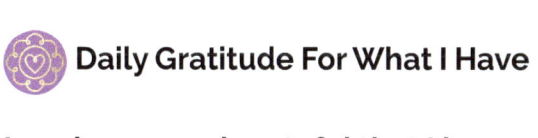 **Daily Gratitude For What I Have**   Date..........................

I am happy and grateful that I have...

Daily Gratitude For What I Want   Date........................

I am happy and grateful that I have manifested...

 I tapped into your higher power and intuition today through meditation ☐

Daily Gratitude For What I Have Date..........................

I am happy and grateful that I have...

Daily Gratitude For What I Want   Date..........................

I am happy and grateful that I have manifested...

....

....

....

....

....

....

....

....

....

....

....

....

....

....

 I tapped into your higher power and intuition today through meditation ☐

Daily Gratitude For What I Have

Date..........................

I am happy and grateful that I have...

Daily Gratitude For What I Want   Date..........................

I am happy and grateful that I have manifested...

....

....

....

....

....

....

....

....

....

....

....

....

....

....

 I tapped into your higher power and intuition today through meditation ☐

Daily Gratitude For What I Have Date..........................

I am happy and grateful that I have...

Daily Gratitude For What I Want Date..........................

I am happy and grateful that I have manifested...

 I tapped into your higher power and intuition today through meditation ☐

"I am sprinkling magic in the air."

Magical Manifesting Month of

....

Things I want to manifest this month...

Daily Gratitude For What I Have

Date..........................

I am happy and grateful that I have...

Daily Gratitude For What I Want Date..........................

I am happy and grateful that I have manifested...

....
....
....
....
....
....
....
....
....
....
....
....
....
....
....
....

 I tapped into your higher power and intuition today through meditation ☐

Daily Gratitude For What I Have　　　Date..........................

I am happy and grateful that I have...

Daily Gratitude For What I Want   Date..........................

I am happy and grateful that I have manifested...

 I tapped into your higher power and intuition today through meditation ☐

 **Daily Gratitude For What I Have**   Date..........................

I am happy and grateful that I have...

Daily Gratitude For What I Want   Date..........................

I am happy and grateful that I have manifested...

....
....
....
....
....
....
....
....
....
....
....
....
....
....
....

 I tapped into your higher power and intuition today through meditation ☐

Daily Gratitude For What I Have   Date..........................

I am happy and grateful that I have...

Daily Gratitude For What I Want   Date..........................

I am happy and grateful that I have manifested...

 I tapped into your higher power and intuition today through meditation ☐

Daily Gratitude For What I Have Date..........................

I am happy and grateful that I have...

Daily Gratitude For What I Want   Date..........................

I am happy and grateful that I have manifested...

....
....
....
....
....
....
....
....
....
....
....
....
....
....
....

 I tapped into your higher power and intuition today through meditation ☐

 **Daily Gratitude For What I Have**   Date..........................

I am happy and grateful that I have...

Daily Gratitude For What I Want Date..........................

I am happy and grateful that I have manifested...

....
....
....
....
....
....
....
....
....
....
....
....
....
....
....

 I tapped into your higher power and intuition today through meditation ☐

 **Daily Gratitude For What I Have**   Date………………………

I am happy and grateful that I have…

Daily Gratitude For What I Want   Date..........................

I am happy and grateful that I have manifested...

....

....

....

....

....

....

....

....

....

....

....

....

....

....

 I tapped into your higher power and intuition today through meditation ☐

Daily Gratitude For What I Have

Date..........................

I am happy and grateful that I have...

Daily Gratitude For What I Want   Date..........................

I am happy and grateful that I have manifested...

....
....
....
....
....
....
....
....
....
....
....
....
....
....
....

 I tapped into your higher power and intuition today through meditation ☐

Daily Gratitude For What I Have   Date...........................

I am happy and grateful that I have...

Daily Gratitude For What I Want   Date..........................

I am happy and grateful that I have manifested...

 I tapped into your higher power and intuition today through meditation ☐

Daily Gratitude For What I Have

Date..........................

I am happy and grateful that I have...

Daily Gratitude For What I Want   Date..........................

I am happy and grateful that I have manifested...

 I tapped into your higher power and intuition today through meditation ☐

"I attract gifts of prosperity."

Magical Manifesting Month of

Things I want to manifest this month...

Daily Gratitude For What I Have   Date..........................

I am happy and grateful that I have...

Daily Gratitude For What I Want　　　Date..........................

I am happy and grateful that I have manifested...

....

....

....

....

....

....

....

....

....

....

....

....

....

....

....

 I tapped into your higher power and intuition today through meditation ☐

Daily Gratitude For What I Have Date..........................

I am happy and grateful that I have...

Daily Gratitude For What I Want   Date..........................

I am happy and grateful that I have manifested...

....
....
....
....
....
....
....
....
....
....
....
....
....
....
....

 I tapped into your higher power and intuition today through meditation ☐

Daily Gratitude For What I Have　　　　　Date..........................

I am happy and grateful that I have...

Daily Gratitude For What I Want   Date..........................

I am happy and grateful that I have manifested...

_____

_____

_____

_____

_____

_____

_____

_____

_____

_____

_____

_____

_____

_____

_____

 I tapped into your higher power and intuition today through meditation ☐

 **Daily Gratitude For What I Have** Date........................

I am happy and grateful that I have...

Daily Gratitude For What I Want   Date..........................

I am happy and grateful that I have manifested...

....

....

....

....

....

....

....

....

....

....

....

....

....

....

 I tapped into your higher power and intuition today through meditation ☐

 **Daily Gratitude For What I Have**   Date..........................

I am happy and grateful that I have...

Daily Gratitude For What I Want   Date..........................

I am happy and grateful that I have manifested...

....
....
....
....
....
....
....
....
....
....
....
....
....
....
....

 I tapped into your higher power and intuition today through meditation ☐

 **Daily Gratitude For What I Have**   Date..........................

I am happy and grateful that I have...

Daily Gratitude For What I Want Date..........................

I am happy and grateful that I have manifested...

....

....

....

....

....

....

....

....

....

....

....

....

....

 I tapped into your higher power and intuition today through meditation ☐

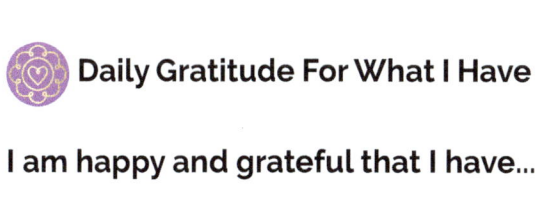 **Daily Gratitude For What I Have**   Date..........................

I am happy and grateful that I have...

Daily Gratitude For What I Want   Date..........................

I am happy and grateful that I have manifested...

 I tapped into your higher power and intuition today through meditation ☐

Daily Gratitude For What I Have   Date..........................

I am happy and grateful that I have...

Daily Gratitude For What I Want   Date..........................

I am happy and grateful that I have manifested...

 I tapped into your higher power and intuition today through meditation ☐

 **Daily Gratitude For What I Have**   **Date**..........................

I am happy and grateful that I have...

Daily Gratitude For What I Want

Date..........................

I am happy and grateful that I have manifested...

 I tapped into your higher power and intuition today through meditation ☐

Daily Gratitude For What I Have Date..........................

I am happy and grateful that I have...

Daily Gratitude For What I Want   Date..........................

I am happy and grateful that I have manifested...

 I tapped into your higher power and intuition today through meditation ☐

"Prosperity is within me."

Magical Manifesting Month of

Things I want to manifest this month...

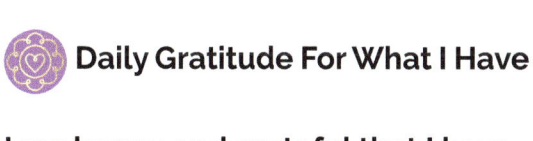 **Daily Gratitude For What I Have**   Date..........................

I am happy and grateful that I have...

Daily Gratitude For What I Want   Date..........................

I am happy and grateful that I have manifested...

_____

_____

_____

_____

_____

_____

_____

_____

_____

_____

_____

_____

_____

_____

 I tapped into your higher power and intuition today through meditation ☐

Daily Gratitude For What I Have Date..........................

I am happy and grateful that I have...

Daily Gratitude For What I Want   Date..........................

I am happy and grateful that I have manifested...

 I tapped into your higher power and intuition today through meditation ☐

Daily Gratitude For What I Have   Date..........................

I am happy and grateful that I have...

Daily Gratitude For What I Want Date........................

I am happy and grateful that I have manifested...

 I tapped into your higher power and intuition today through meditation ☐

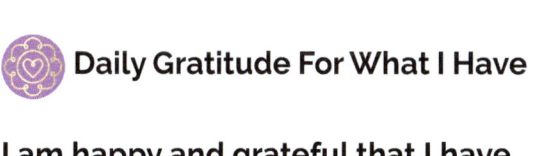 **Daily Gratitude For What I Have**   Date..........................

I am happy and grateful that I have...

Daily Gratitude For What I Want   Date..........................

I am happy and grateful that I have manifested...

....

....

....

....

....

....

....

....

....

....

....

....

....

....

 I tapped into your higher power and intuition today through meditation ☐

Daily Gratitude For What I Have   Date..........................

I am happy and grateful that I have...

Daily Gratitude For What I Want   Date..........................

I am happy and grateful that I have manifested...

....
....
....
....
....
....
....
....
....
....
....
....
....
....

 I tapped into your higher power and intuition today through meditation ☐

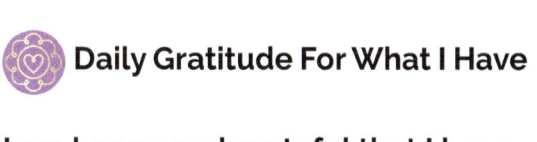

Daily Gratitude For What I Have

Date..........................

I am happy and grateful that I have...

Daily Gratitude For What I Want Date..........................

I am happy and grateful that I have manifested...

....
....
....
....
....
....
....
....
....
....
....
....
....
....
....

 I tapped into your higher power and intuition today through meditation ☐

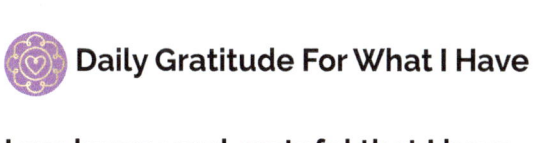
Daily Gratitude For What I Have   Date..........................

I am happy and grateful that I have...

Daily Gratitude For What I Want   Date..........................

I am happy and grateful that I have manifested...

_____

_____

_____

_____

_____

_____

_____

_____

_____

_____

_____

_____

_____

_____

_____

 I tapped into your higher power and intuition today through meditation ☐

Daily Gratitude For What I Have   Date..........................

I am happy and grateful that I have...

Daily Gratitude For What I Want Date..........................

I am happy and grateful that I have manifested...

....
....
....
....
....
....
....
....
....
....
....
....
....
....
....
....
....

 I tapped into your higher power and intuition today through meditation ☐

Daily Gratitude For What I Have Date..........................

I am happy and grateful that I have...

Daily Gratitude For What I Want   Date........................

I am happy and grateful that I have manifested...

....

....

....

....

....

....

....

....

....

....

....

....

....

....

 I tapped into your higher power and intuition today through meditation ☐

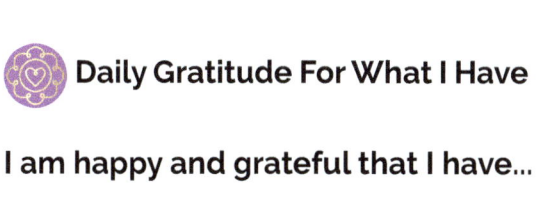 **Daily Gratitude For What I Have**   **Date**..........................

I am happy and grateful that I have...

Daily Gratitude For What I Want   Date..........................

I am happy and grateful that I have manifested...

....

....

....

....

....

....

....

....

....

....

....

....

....

....

....

 I tapped into your higher power and intuition today through meditation ☐

"I am the source of my prosperity."

Magical Manifesting Month of

Things I want to manifest this month...

Daily Gratitude For What I Have Date..........................

I am happy and grateful that I have...

Daily Gratitude For What I Want   Date..........................

I am happy and grateful that I have manifested...

....
....
....
....
....
....
....
....
....
....
....
....
....
....
....

 I tapped into your higher power and intuition today through meditation ☐

Daily Gratitude For What I Have

Date..........................

I am happy and grateful that I have...

Daily Gratitude For What I Want   Date..........................

I am happy and grateful that I have manifested...

 I tapped into your higher power and intuition today through meditation ☐

 **Daily Gratitude For What I Have** Date..........................

I am happy and grateful that I have...

Daily Gratitude For What I Want   Date.........................

I am happy and grateful that I have manifested...

 I tapped into your higher power and intuition today through meditation ☐

 **Daily Gratitude For What I Have**   Date..........................

I am happy and grateful that I have...

Daily Gratitude For What I Want   Date..........................

I am happy and grateful that I have manifested...

....

....

....

....

....

....

....

....

....

....

....

....

....

....

 I tapped into your higher power and intuition today through meditation ☐

Daily Gratitude For What I Have   Date..........................

I am happy and grateful that I have...

Daily Gratitude For What I Want   Date........................

I am happy and grateful that I have manifested...

....
....
....
....
....
....
....
....
....
....
....
....
....
....
....

 I tapped into your higher power and intuition today through meditation ☐

 **Daily Gratitude For What I Have**   Date..........................

I am happy and grateful that I have...

Daily Gratitude For What I Want   Date........................

I am happy and grateful that I have manifested...

  I tapped into your higher power and intuition today through meditation ☐

Daily Gratitude For What I Have   Date..........................

I am happy and grateful that I have...

Daily Gratitude For What I Want   Date..........................

I am happy and grateful that I have manifested...

....

....

....

....

....

....

....

....

....

....

....

....

....

....

....

 I tapped into your higher power and intuition today through meditation ☐

 **Daily Gratitude For What I Have** Date...........................

I am happy and grateful that I have...

Daily Gratitude For What I Want

Date..........................

I am happy and grateful that I have manifested...

 I tapped into your higher power and intuition today through meditation ☐

 **Daily Gratitude For What I Have**   **Date**..........................

I am happy and grateful that I have...

Daily Gratitude For What I Want   Date..........................

I am happy and grateful that I have manifested...

_____

_____

_____

_____

_____

_____

_____

_____

_____

_____

_____

_____

_____

_____

 I tapped into your higher power and intuition today through meditation ☐

Daily Gratitude For What I Have

Date..........................

I am happy and grateful that I have...

Daily Gratitude For What I Want   Date..........................

I am happy and grateful that I have manifested...

....
....
....
....
....
....
....
....
....
....
....
....
....
....

 I tapped into your higher power and intuition today through meditation ☐

"I have limitless power to attract my desires."

Magical Manifesting Month of

....

Things I want to manifest this month...

 **Daily Gratitude For What I Have** Date..........................

I am happy and grateful that I have...

Daily Gratitude For What I Want   Date..........................

I am happy and grateful that I have manifested...

....
....
....
....
....
....
....
....
....
....
....
....
....
....

 I tapped into your higher power and intuition today through meditation ☐

 **Daily Gratitude For What I Have**   Date..........................

I am happy and grateful that I have...

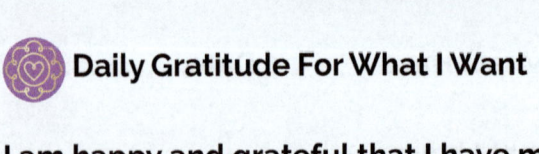 **Daily Gratitude For What I Want**   Date..........................

I am happy and grateful that I have manifested...

....
....
....
....
....
....
....
....
....
....
....
....
....
....
....
....

 I tapped into your higher power and intuition today through meditation ☐

 **Daily Gratitude For What I Have**   Date..........................

I am happy and grateful that I have...

Daily Gratitude For What I Want Date........................

I am happy and grateful that I have manifested...

 I tapped into your higher power and intuition today through meditation ☐

 **Daily Gratitude For What I Have**　　　　Date...........................

I am happy and grateful that I have...

Daily Gratitude For What I Want Date..........................

I am happy and grateful that I have manifested...

 I tapped into your higher power and intuition today through meditation ☐

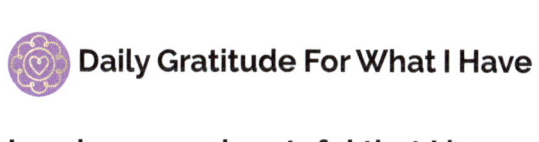

Daily Gratitude For What I Have

Date..........................

I am happy and grateful that I have...

Daily Gratitude For What I Want

Date..........................

I am happy and grateful that I have manifested...

....
....
....
....
....
....
....
....
....
....
....
....
....
....

 I tapped into your higher power and intuition today through meditation ☐

Daily Gratitude For What I Have

Date..........................

I am happy and grateful that I have...

Daily Gratitude For What I Want   Date..........................

I am happy and grateful that I have manifested...

 I tapped into your higher power and intuition today through meditation ☐

 **Daily Gratitude For What I Have**   **Date**..........................

I am happy and grateful that I have...

Daily Gratitude For What I Want   Date..........................

I am happy and grateful that I have manifested...

....

....

....

....

....

....

....

....

....

....

....

....

....

....

....

....

  I tapped into your higher power and intuition today through meditation ☐

Daily Gratitude For What I Have   Date..........................

I am happy and grateful that I have...

Daily Gratitude For What I Want   Date..........................

I am happy and grateful that I have manifested...

....
....
....
....
....
....
....
....
....
....
....
....
....
....

 I tapped into your higher power and intuition today through meditation ☐

 **Daily Gratitude For What I Have** **Date**..........................

I am happy and grateful that I have...

Daily Gratitude For What I Want   Date..........................

I am happy and grateful that I have manifested...

_____

_____

_____

_____

_____

_____

_____

_____

_____

_____

_____

_____

_____

_____

 I tapped into your higher power and intuition today through meditation ☐

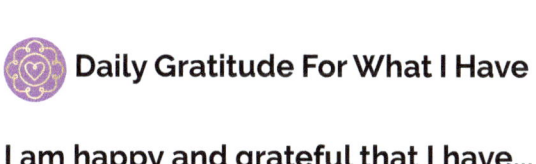 **Daily Gratitude For What I Have**   Date..........................

I am happy and grateful that I have...

Daily Gratitude For What I Want   Date..........................

I am happy and grateful that I have manifested...

 I tapped into your higher power and intuition today through meditation ☐

"I live in joy, happiness and contentment."

Magical Manifesting Month of

Things I want to manifest this month...

Daily Gratitude For What I Have   Date..........................

I am happy and grateful that I have...

Daily Gratitude For What I Want   Date........................

I am happy and grateful that I have manifested...

_____

_____

_____

_____

_____

_____

_____

_____

_____

_____

_____

_____

_____

_____

   I tapped into your higher power and intuition today through meditation   ☐

 **Daily Gratitude For What I Have**   Date..........................

I am happy and grateful that I have...

Daily Gratitude For What I Want Date........................

I am happy and grateful that I have manifested...

....
....
....
....
....
....
....
....
....
....
....
....
....
....
....

 I tapped into your higher power and intuition today through meditation ☐

 **Daily Gratitude For What I Have**   Date..........................

I am happy and grateful that I have...

Daily Gratitude For What I Want   Date........................

I am happy and grateful that I have manifested...

 I tapped into your higher power and intuition today through meditation ☐

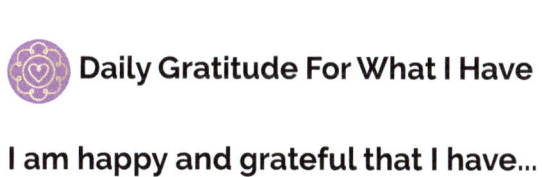 **Daily Gratitude For What I Have**   Date..........................

I am happy and grateful that I have...

Daily Gratitude For What I Want   Date..........................

I am happy and grateful that I have manifested...

_____
_____
_____
_____
_____
_____
_____
_____
_____
_____
_____
_____
_____
_____
_____

 I tapped into your higher power and intuition today through meditation ☐

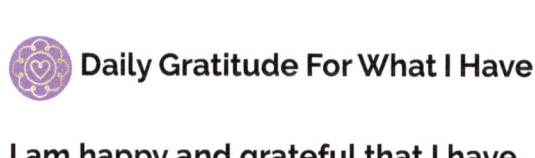 **Daily Gratitude For What I Have**   Date..........................

I am happy and grateful that I have...

Daily Gratitude For What I Want

Date..........................

I am happy and grateful that I have manifested...

....
....
....
....
....
....
....
....
....
....
....
....
....
....
....

 I tapped into your higher power and intuition today through meditation ☐

 **Daily Gratitude For What I Have**

Date..........................

I am happy and grateful that I have...

Daily Gratitude For What I Want   Date..........................

I am happy and grateful that I have manifested...

....

....

....

....

....

....

....

....

....

....

....

....

....

....

   I tapped into your higher power and intuition today through meditation ☐

 **Daily Gratitude For What I Have**   **Date**..........................

I am happy and grateful that I have...

Daily Gratitude For What I Want Date..........................

I am happy and grateful that I have manifested...

  I tapped into your higher power and intuition today through meditation ☐

 **Daily Gratitude For What I Have**   Date..........................

I am happy and grateful that I have...

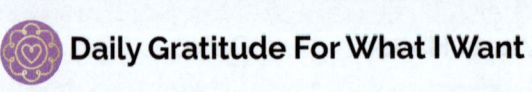 **Daily Gratitude For What I Want**   Date..........................

I am happy and grateful that I have manifested...

....
....
....
....
....
....
....
....
....
....
....
....
....
....

 I tapped into your higher power and intuition today through meditation ☐

Daily Gratitude For What I Have   Date..........................

I am happy and grateful that I have...

Daily Gratitude For What I Want   Date........................

I am happy and grateful that I have manifested...

_____

_____

_____

_____

_____

_____

_____

_____

_____

_____

_____

_____

_____

 I tapped into your higher power and intuition today through meditation ☐

Daily Gratitude For What I Have Date..........................

I am happy and grateful that I have...

Daily Gratitude For What I Want Date........................

I am happy and grateful that I have manifested...

....
....
....
....
....
....
....
....
....
....
....
....
....
....
....
....

 I tapped into your higher power and intuition today through meditation ☐

Mega Journaling

Lightning Source UK Ltd.
Milton Keynes UK
UKHW021023030120
356312UK00001B/8/P